THE
MAYAS

HISTORY • ART • ARCHAEOLOGY

Cover:
The Observatory,
Chichén Itzá
Photograpy: Bonechi Archives

Text: Susana Vogel

Photographs:
Enrique Franco Torrijos
Irmgard Groth
Walter Reuter
Ruth D. Lechuga
Guillermo Aldana
Vicente Santiago
Bonechi Archives
Monclem Archives
◖▲〗︎︎NAH ❀

Drawing by:
Heraclio Ramírez

Translation by: David B. Castledine

© 1995 by Monclem Ediciones, S.A. de C.V.
   Leibnitz 31, Col. Anzures 11590
   México, D.F., México.

Printed in Mexico
Impreso en México
ISBN 968-6434-39-9

CONTENTS

Surrounded by the Chiapas rain forest in Mexico stands Yaxchilán, a Maya city that was at its height in the Late Classic period.

Geography of the Maya World

In pre-Hispanic times the Mayas occupied a wide region with different climates and varied vegetation: mountains and plains, rain forest and arid areas; lands with rivers, lakes and waterfalls, and long stretches of seacoast. The Maya area covered what are now the states of Quintana Roo, Campeche, Yucatan, Tabasco and eastern Chiapas in Mexico; Guatemala, Belize, and the western part of Honduras and El Salvador in Central America.

There are three large natural areas within this region: the first, the Southern area, includes the Pacific coast, the Highlands of Guatemala, part of Chiapas and of El Salvador. Several volcanic lakes lie on the high plateau, for example Amatitlán, Atitlán and Izabal, together with Lake Guaja between Guatemala and El Salvador and in the east, Lake Ayarza. All this area is rich in fruit trees and timber and houses a wide variety of animals and birds, including the quetzal, which the Mayas held sacred in the belief that it was a representative of the gods.

The second or Central area is the largest, covering the interior basin of the Petén Department in Guatemala, part of Honduras and Chiapas, Tabasco and the southern part of the Yucatan peninsula. This is an area of tropical forest with a hot, humid climate containing several rivers, the most important of them being the Grijalva, which empties into the Gulf of Mexico, and the Hondo, Sarstún and Mopán flowing into the Caribbean.

This region of rain forest and pasture is extremely rich in hardwoods such as cedar and also contains the most varied fauna in the Maya area.

The third, or Northern, zone is the northern area of the Yucatan peninsula, its flat limestone expanses broken only by La Sierrita or Puuc Hills running from Campeche to Yucatan that are 200 meters above sea level. This is an extremely dry region with scrub vegetation and yet a

The Maya area contains different natural regions, including this flat dry zone of the Yucatan Peninsula.

surprising number of medicinal herbs. There are three small rivers, the Lagartos, Hondo and Champotón, and one lake, Bacalar.

Rainwater seeps down quickly in this limestone area to form underground deposits in caves; when the cave roof

A wide range of fauna lived in the Maya area. Some served as food and others provided skins and feathers to clothe and decorate the headdresses of high ranking persons. The jaguar was very important, being associated with the power of the ruling class and with religion.

collapses, wells called cenotes appear. These have been very important in the region's history, providing water for the population. The ancient Mayas founded cities near them; one of the most important is Chichén Itzá. Human beings, rubber, jade, vessels, beads and gold artifacts were thrown into its Sacred Cenote as offerings to Chaac, the god of Rain.

6

Origins • History

Originally the Mayas were different groups sharing a common historical tradition. As a result their culture traits were similar, though there were specific local variations. They had similar physical characteristics and spoke languages belonging to the same linguistic stock.

Studies of the Maya language have led to the conclusion that around 2500 B.C. there was a proto-Maya group living in the area of what is now Huehuetenango, Guatemala. The members of this group spoke what researchers have named Proto-Maya, which in the course of time subdivided into different Mayance languages. The speakers of these languages later migrated and settled on the different sites that would afterwards define the Maya area and give rise to their advanced culture.

These migrations caused both the separation of the different groups and their contact with other cultures. This has led to various theories about where the Maya culture originated. According to some researchers it was in the north of Tabasco and southern Veracruz, where these groups intermingled with Olmecs. A second theory inclines toward the opinion that it first arose in the mountains of Guatemala: the groups created an agricultural society, growing corn, and then spread north and west, where they were influenced by other cultures. particularly the Olmecs. Olmec civilization is regarded as the mother culture because it provided the basic elements for the development of other important cultures in Mesoamerica. Some of the most important cultural elements that the Olmecs left to the Mayas were architectural features and an elementary number and calendar system that later evolved into the accurate Maya calendar.

The chronology of the Maya culture is similar to that of all Mesoamerica, although the sequence is more precise, thanks to the interpretation of its time glyphs. These have been correlated with the modern calendar, and on this basis J. Eric S. Thompson established the following periods:

Formative or pre-Classic: 500 B.C. to 325 A.D. Maya culture begins to take shape, shown particularly in anthropomorphic clay figurines with the typical physical features of people at that time. This can be seen in the decoration of their first buildings.

The physical appearance of the Mayas can be seen from this remarkable stucco model from Palenque, Chiapas, Mexico.

Classic: 325 to 925 A.D. This is divided into the *Early Classic,* from 325 to 625 A.D. when external influences ended and typical features appeared such as the corbel arch and the practice of recording historical dates with glyphs. The second subdivision is the *Flowering,* from 625 to 800 A.D., when culture was at its height in mathematics, astronomy, hieroglyphic writing, pottery, sculpture and architecture. The *Collapse* lasted from 800 to 825 A.D. when the culture declined and ceremonial centers were abandoned.

Transitional or Interregnum: from 925 to 975 A.D. This marks a fall in culture almost to the level of the Formative period.

Maya-Toltec or Mexica: from 975 to 1200 A.D. This was

Monumental stone head belonging to the Olmec culture, which influenced Maya culture considerably. La Venta, Tabasco, Mexico.

Pyramid of the Sun, Teotihuacan. The influence of this great city on the Central Plateau also reached the Maya area.

the period when influences arrived with Nahua speaking groups of Toltec culture from central Mexico; the cult of Quetzalcóatl (Kukulcán in Maya) arose. Alliances were formed between towns governed by Maya families and those ruled by families of Nahua origin.

Mexica Absorption: 1200 to 1540 A.D. A period when several conflicts arose, the alliances were broken and warfare divided the population and impoverished the culture further. When the Spanish reached the Maya region the great ceremonial centers were already abandoned and the culture was in complete decline. The first contact was in 1511, when a ship on Valdivia's expedition from Panama to Santo Domingo sank. Two survivors, Gonzalo Guerrero and Jerónimo de Aguilar, were taken prisoner by the Mayas.

Atlantes from the city of Tula, Mexico. Toltec culture reached the Yucatan Peninsula by conquest.

Guerrero adopted their customs, married, and produced a family. He even fought with the Mayas against his countrymen. Meanwhile, Aguilar remained a slave and in 1519 joined Cortés and was one of his interpreters during the conquest of Mexico.

Yucatan was discovered by Francisco Hernández de Córdoba in 1517; between 1523 and 1525, Pedro de Alvarado conquered the area that is now Guatemala. In 1526, Francisco de Montejo the Elder began the conquest of the Yucatan peninsula and Francisco Montejo the Younger finished his father's work, founding Merida in 1542 and Valladolid in 1543. The last refuge of the ancient Mayas was Tayasal, a city on lake Petén Itzá, not conquered by the Spanish until 1697.

Social organization

In the Early pre-Classic period Maya society was composed of family groups that shared the same language, customs and territory. They gathered together to cultivate the land, to fish, hunt and collect food for survival. Later, when agriculture was more developed, irrigation systems were built and crops diversified, some of them to be traded. The population grew considerably, great ceremonial centers were begun, and the ordinary people settled around them. The different social classes arose as a result of the

Left. The supreme ruler, Halach Uinic, was the head of all governors or Bacabes of the lands and cities under his power. He is followed by the nobles and warriors, craftsmen, and finally peasants.

A Maya lord wearing jewels and an elaborate headdress. Clay figurine from the island of Jaina, Campeche, Mexico.

division of labor.

The number of cities and ceremonial centers increased in the Classic period. In them lived the ruling class, devoted to government, the priests and specialists in the arts of magic, warriors and merchants, as well as the architects who were responsible for planning temples, palaces and public buildings, astronomers —who observed the movement of the heavenly bodies and tried to discover the harmony of the Universe and the recurring cycles of time— and the scribes, whose job was to record important historical events, mythical and religious beliefs, the genealogies of rulers and the exploits of the warriors in codices, using a complex system of hieroglyphic writing.

13

At an intermediate level there were the builders, the servants of the ruling class, potters and other craftsmen. Finally, there was the lower class formed of fishermen, hunters and farmers, who lived on the outskirts of the cities and ceremonial centers. There were also slaves, called *pentacoob* in Maya, who were generally prisoners of war, the children of slaves, or orphans.

At the end of the Classic period and throughout the Postclassic, this division into social classes continued although religious and political powers, formerly in the hands of a single person, were divided. The rulers were headed by the Halach Uinic (True Man), and the priests by the Ahau Can (Lord Serpent) each with defined tasks.

The Maya-Toltec or Mexica period saw the arrival of Nahua speaking groups, bringing Toltec culture from central Mexico to the Yucatan peninsula. They exerted their influences on both material culture and customs. Finally, in the period of Mexica Absorption, wars and uprisings led to the destruction of social organization and the abandoning of cities.

Left. Lintel 53 from Yaxchilán, Chiapas, carved with the Halach Uinic handing over a scepter, a symbol of power, to a noblewoman. Classic period.

Maya peasant huts in Yucatan still keep the same features as in pre-Hispanic times, as can be seen from this carving on a frieze at Uxmal.

Trade

Trade was an important activity on the regional level and with more distant areas of Maya zone and Mesoamerica. Trade routes were established between different places for transporting vanilla, rubber, feathers, jaguar skins, tobacco and honey; for moving shells, dried fish and pearls from the Gulf Coast to central Mexico, the Chiapas highlands, Guatemala, El Salvador, Costa Rica and Panama. This trade was under the supervision of merchants belonging to the nobility, whose products were carried by slaves along land routes or sent by river and sea in large canoes. Trade was usually carried out by exchanging different products, although cacao beans were also used as currency.

Tulum on the Mexican Caribbean coast was one of the Mayas' most important maritime trading centers. All kinds of products arrived in its cove from other regions.

Above left. Figurine from Jaina of a merchant, identified by his fan. Classic period.

Gold earrings found at Gumarcah, Guatemala. These were imported from other regions, since the Mayas were not goldsmiths.

Religion

Religion was of key importance in the Maya culture, permeating all aspects of life. Priests had great influence among both the elite and the ordinary people sincethey directed the ceremonies and rites to propitiate the supernatural, which was ruled by the different gods.

The gods embodied natural forces, the celestial bodies, the rain that was so necessary for survival, and death. The

Left. Funerary mask of jade, shell and pyrite. The stone in its mouth represents the eternal spirit. Tikal, Guatemala. Classic period.

The masks decorating the Codz Pop at Kabáh, Yucatan, represent Chaac, the highly venerated god of Rain.

gods were worshiped with offerings, festivals, penitence and self-mutilation, and included *Chaac,* god of Rain and Lightning; *Hunab Ku,* the Creator god, *Itzamná,* lord of the Heavens, *Ixchel,* goddess of the Moon and Childbirth, *Ik,* god of Wind, *Ek Chuac,* patron of cacao and god of War, and *Ah Puch,* the god of Death, who was also known as *Yum Kimil* or *Kisin.* Later, during the era of Toltec influence from the Central Plateau, the god Quetzalcóatl —the feathered serpent— was worshiped, who was given the name of Kukulcán in Maya.

The gods were also symbolized by animals: for example, rain as a snake, the sun as a jaguar or macaw, and death by an owl or bat. Thus, in carvings, paintings and monuments, deities may be shown as fabulous beings that incorporate animal and human forms decorated with plant motifs or else with fangs, claws and feathers.

The Mayas thought of the Universe as formed by three levels: Heaven, the Earth and the Underworld. The Sky

Human sacrifices were offered
to the gods in the Sacred
Cenote of Chichén Itzá.

Right. Priest of the Rain god
holding a vessel and a human
heart. Mayapán.

was divided into thirteen planes, inhabited by the celestial
bodies —which were gods— and Itzamná, the supreme
god who gave life to all the cosmos. They thought of the
Earth as a flat plate floating on water, but also as an
enormous crocodile with vegetation on its back. The
Underworld consisted of nine layers, the lowest being the
realm of Ah Puch, god of Death, who was usually repre-
sented as a human skeleton. Sky, Earth and Underworld
were in turn each divided into four sectors, corresponding
to the cardinal points. Each of these had its own color
value, and a ceiba (held to be a sacred tree) of the same
color stood there. At the center stood the great mother
ceiba, the hub of the world.

They believed that the gods had created and destroyed the
universe several times. On each occasion, man had pro-
gressed in his evolution until he arrived at the Maya era.
Here, man had been made from corn dough and had the
obligation to honor and feed the gods with offerings and
sacrifices so that they in turn would ensure that the universe
would continue to exist.

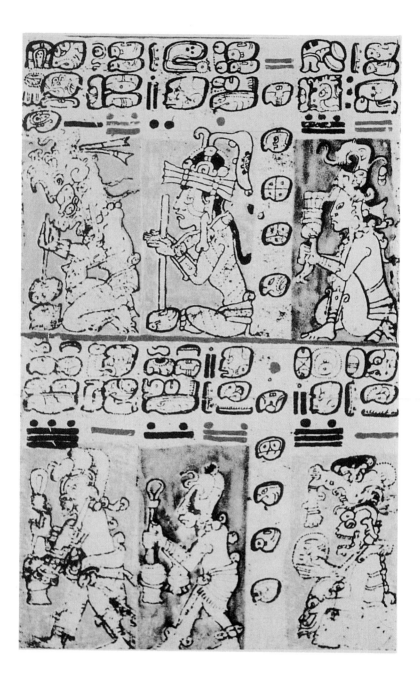

Page 6 of the Dresden Codex, the most
beautiful of the Maya codices, showing
gods and priests together with
hieroglyphs and bar-and-dot numerals.

*Ballgame player wearing hip protector.
Classic Period.*

The ballgame

The ballgame, in Maya *pok ta pok*, was a remarkable rite practiced in several parts of Mesoamerica, and there were courts for it in almost all Maya cities. Their ground plan was I shaped, bounded by either sloping or vertical walls with the targets on them and an area for spectators on top. The courts were built in the ceremonial centers and the walls were carved with reliefs alluding to the mythological and religious significance of the game, since it was associated with myth and the universe. The ball reproduced the movement of the stars in the sky and two opposing teams often symbolized the struggle between day and night or between the gods of the Underworld and those of the Sky. The game was often accompanied by ritual beheading to ensure the earth's fertility. Some experts say that the captain of the winning team was executed, others that this was the fate of the losers, and yet others that prisoners of war were the ones sacrificed.

23

*Hoop target from
the Ballcourt at
Uxmal, Yucatan.*

*Ballcourt at Chichén Itzá.
Post Classic period.*

*Right. One of the benches in the Ballcourt of Chichén Itzá is
carved with a scene of a player being ritually beheaded. Blood
spurts from his neck in the form of serpents. The symbol of
death is on his left.*

However, the game was also an entertainment that showed
off the players' skill: the solid rubber ball was propelled
with the hip from one side of the court to the other to score.
At the same time the object was to shoot it through one
of the stone hoops jutting from the side walls of the court.
Because this was extremely difficult and only managed
very occasionally it brought the team immediate victory.
The spectators would bet on their favorite team, showing
that the game also had its non-religious side.

Writing • Mathematics

Maya writing and numerical system originated in concepts inherited from the Olmecs. The hieroglyphic writing has both ideographic and phonetic elements that have not been completely deciphered yet, and some glyphs had two forms that were interchangeable. They were used to write texts and calendar information in murals, stele and codices, recording the history, myths and genealogy of important rulers.

In mathematics, number symbols were given values according to their position, and the concept of zero was used. The system was vigesimal and the Mayas could write the numbers from 0 to 19 in the first (bottom) position. The ideograms or number symbols used were basically three: a dot for one, a bar for five and a stylized shell for zero, and the different numbers sere written by combining them. There were also 20 ideograms that often replaced the dots and bars.

Glyph for the name of the god 1 Ahau on a stone tablet in Temple XIV, Palenque.

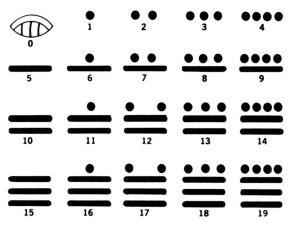

Bar-and-dot number symbols. Their value depended on their position.

 0
 1
2
3
4

5
6
7
8
9

 10
 11
 12
 13
 14

 15
 16
 17
 18
 18
 19
 19

Maya "head numerals". These only exist for 0 to 19.

27

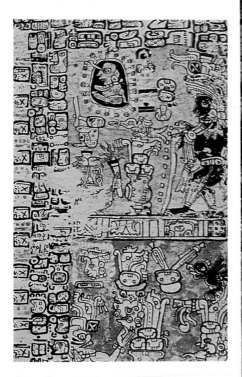

Page from the Madrid Codex
showing a Maya astronomer
observing the night sky.

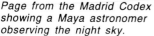

Astronomy

Astronomy was very important to the Mayas. They constructed special buildings for observing the stars, such as the Caracol at Chichén Itzá and Group E at Uaxactún. From these they noted the appearance and disappearance of celestial bodies in the different seasons. They recorded the annual cycle of the sun as 365 days and also the lunar cycle with only a small margin of error. They drew up tables for the solar eclipses that would occur in a period of 33 years, calculating the cycles of Mars, Jupiter and Saturn. They also plotted the movements of certain constellations such as the Pleiades, which they called *Tzab* (serpent's rattle) and Gemini or *Ac* (turtle).

The Caracol or Observatory at Chichén Itzá. The Mayas studied the stars from the round tower.

They used this knowledge to create two calendars. One was the solar called *Haab* with 365 days divided into 18 months of 20 days each plus 5 extra ones named *uayeb*. The other was the ritual calendar or *Tzolkin* of 260 days, designated by 20 signs and 13 numbers, which was used to determine the festivals of the gods and predict human destinies. Generally the two were combined, and the Mayas recorder the same date in both the *Tzolkin* and the *Haab*. To fix a date in a certain year there was a new combination, and 18,980 days would have to go by before the combination was repeated, i.e 52 solar years and 73 ritual years. Mayanists have named this the Calendar Round.

Jade mask from the tomb in the Temple of the Inscriptions at Palenque. Classic period.

Beautiful stucco head portraying King Pacal of Palenque, found in his tomb. Classic Period.

Sculpture

Maya artists used basalt, obsidian and silex chisels, mallets and hammers made of flint and wood, and obsidian knives to produce their sculpture. With these tools they carved the blocks of limestone that were taken to the site of the monument with ritual, mythical historical and symbolic motifs, usually accompanied by calendar glyphs.

Their sculptures show the typical symbolism of the Maya culture that in time gave the buildings an air of serenity, balanced proportions, dimension and depth. They depicted deities, governors and priests wearing elaborate costumes, and various personalities. Stele mark important dates; carved monoliths and different sculptures were placed in squares, courts and temple entrances. Designs were also carved on vertical walls, columns, lintels and ceremonial chambers.

This figurine full of movement from Jonuta,
Tabasco, Mexico, exemplifies Maya sculpture.

Jade pectoral carved with a governor opposite a snake and a dwarf. Nebaj, Guatemala.

Right. Stele B at Copán, Honduras, portraying a governor wearing an elaborate headdress.

In the Early Classic, stele were carved with human figures, both full face and in profile, and different zoomorphic figures. Clay figurines were at first coarse, such as those produced in the 1st and 2nd centuries A.D., but gradually became more refined until they reached the degree of perfection shown by those from the island of Jaina in Campeche.

Figures were produced later in wood, and then in stone, stucco, obsidian and jade. In the Classic period, human figures are usually shown on foot and in profile; later, seated figures were made. The peak was reached during the Flowering of the Classic period.

When the Collapse came, artistic expression declined and sculpture became purely decorative to be followed by influence from the Toltec culture in Yucatan shortly afterwards. During the Postclassic there was a slight reawakening in sculpture, though generally speaking it did not reach the importance it had in earlier periods.

33

Snail shaped vessel decorated with raised hieroglyphs. Classic period.

Pottery

The Mayas made pottery for both domestic and ceremonial and ritual use. They used molds, worked directly with lumps of clay or built vessels with rolled strips or balls, drying the finished pieces in the open air. Shapes varied widely: figurines, urns, incense burners, drinking vessels, cooking pots, etc, and different styles, which experts have grouped into several phases. These are the *Formative or Preclassic,* characterized by rudimentary objects of red or gray clay with monochrome designs; the *Early Classic,* when techniques developed considerably, shapes diversified and colors were used to decorate figures. In the *Middle Classic* pieces were painted or incised with multicolored geometric designs on a yellow or orange background. The *Late Classic* marks the high point of pottery, with figures realistically painted on surfaces in white, red and yellow, often in combination with calendar glyphs. Finally, Yucatan arose as a pottery center in the *Postclassic* and new techniques were created, but this did not rival the splendor of the previous period.

*Vessel from Altar de Sacrificios, Guatemala
decorated with hieroglyphs and a shaman in a
jaguar skin performing ritual dances with a
serpent.*

Painting

Painting contains a wide variety of symbolic elements such as masks, serpents, astronomical signs, elaborate feather headdresses and glyphs. Mythical and religious feeling led Maya artists to emphasize the features that supernatural beings had, according to their beliefs

The depiction of human beings was very important, but symbolic attributes were always emphasized. Thus, walls and vessels were painted with warriors, priests and gods in their different colors, with varied costume and ornaments, usually shown participating in ceremonies and rituals.

Mural paintings in temples, tombs and pyramids such as at Tikal, Uxmal. Palenque, Chichén Itzá, Tulum, Yaxchilán, Uaxactún and Bonampak include anthropomorphic and zoomorphic figures. The examples belong to different periods and their state of preservation depends on their age.

Other pictorial forms appear in codices and on pottery, whose colors include the classic "Maya blue".

Left. The murals of Bonampak, Chiapas, are the finest expression of Maya painting. Copy in the National Museum of Anthropology, Mexico City of part of the battle scene decorating Temple 2.

Mural from the Temple of the Frescoes at Tulum. It shows an old goddess carrying images of the god Chaac and a plant with pods, all probably related to the fertility of the earth.

37

Architecture

Buildings were begun in the Formative period, when architecture showed influences from other cultures, particularly Olmec. Later, Maya architecture was affected by mythical and religious ideas. This is why temples and palaces, citadels and ballcourts were built in the center of cities, while the houses of ordinary people stood on the outskirts.

It was in the Classic period that the typical Maya features emerged such as the corbel or Maya arch, superposed

The Palace and Temple of the Inscriptions, Palenque. This city developed an art style of its own in the Classic period.

terraces, moldings, roof crests and columns that in combination gave rise to several distinctive styles known as:
Petén - buildings standing on stepped terraces, thick walls, sloping sections, staircases projecting from the façade, tall roof crests on the rear wall and decoration of stucco masks. This style is found on sites such as Calakmul in Mexico, and Tikal, Piedras Negras and Uaxactún in Guatemala.
Palenque - vertical base platforms, staircases with side ramps, façades decorated with stucco figures, roof crests

Temple of the Great Jaguar or Temple 1 in the magnificent Maya city of Tikal, Guatemala.

on the central wall, temples with two rooms, the rear one being used as a shrine. This style is found at Yaxchilán, Palenque and Bonampak in Mexico, at Copán in Honduras and Quiriguá in Guatemala.

In 1952, a funeral chamber was discovered in the Temple of the Inscriptions at Palenque, and in June 1994, another similarly magnificent one was opened close by.

Río Bec - characterized by the use of stylized pyramidal bases, purely decorative stairways that look like high towers at the sides of the temple and decoration formed of stone mosaic. To be seen at Xpuhil, Río Bec and Hormiguero in Mexico.

Chenes - a style that developed together with Puuc, so the two contain similar elements such as bases with sloping, stepped tiers, roof crests standing on the front part, columns and vertical friezes, and decoration based on stone

General view of Uxmal, one of the centers most typical of the Puuc style.

Detail of the rich carving on the East Building of the Nunnery Quadrangle, Uxmal.

The Castillo is the most outstanding building at Chichén Itzá. Maya-Toltec style.

mosaic forming masks, small columns, latticework, pillar drums and panels. Present at Labná, Kabáh, Uxmal, Sayil, Hochob and Edzná in Mexico. Some of the most beautiful buildings in this style are at Uxmal, such as the Pyramid of the Magician and the Governor's Palace.

Puuc - which differs mainly in the decoration made of stone mosaic on the friezes, not on the entire façade.

Mexica or *Maya-Toltec* - this was the result of Toltec cultural influence, although it retains some Puuc elements. Features are high platforms and sloping walls, staircases with serpent heads at the bottom, and altars decorated with skulls. Chichén Itzá, Tulum and Mayapán in Mexico.

The classic style of the Maya arch is illustrated by the Arch of Labná, Yucatan.

Palace of Sayil in Yucatan. It belongs to the Puuc style and columns are the main element of decoration.

Hut of a Tzotzil family in Chiapas. Different ethnic groups can be identified by their costume.

The Mayas of today

The groups speaking languages belonging to the Maya stock still live in villages in the area where their ancestors created their high culture. They have different economic, social, religious and cultural patterns which at the same time share some common traits.

Their religion combines pre-Hispanic and Roman Catholic beliefs; they worship the gods of nature and perform rituals to control weather and for curing sickness which are directed by specialists in the supernatural; they venerate the saints and celebrate certain saint's days of the Catholic calendar. They also preserve both pre-Hispanic and Colonial elements in their political and religious organization through an elaborate system of positions for serving the community. They live in settlements apart from the village proper with its church and municipal offices at the center, in houses in the surrounding areas.

44

Indian women still use the backstrap loom as they did in pre-Hispanic times.

Maya women of today at a market in the city of Merida, Yucatan.

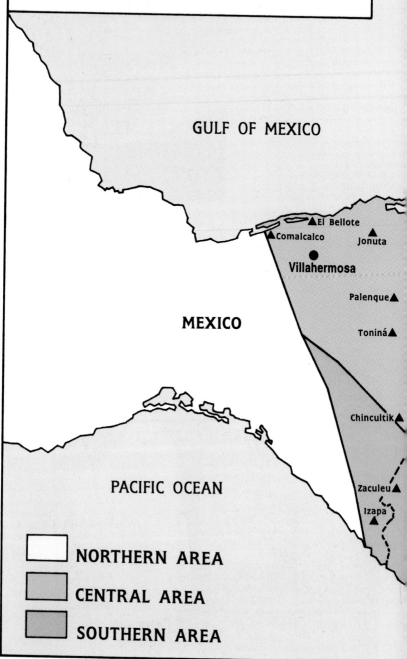

ARCHAEOLOGICAL SITES OF THE MAYA CULTURE IN MEXICO, GUATEMALA, BELIZE AND HONDURAS

GULF OF MEXICO

▲El Bellote
▲Comalcalco
Jonuta ▲

● Villahermosa

Palenque ▲

MEXICO

Toniná ▲

Chincultik ▲

PACIFIC OCEAN

Zaculeu ▲

Izapa ▲

NORTHERN AREA

CENTRAL AREA

SOUTHERN AREA

Isla
Mujeres

▲ Dzibilchaltún

▲ Izamal

● Mérida   Chichén Itzá   El Rey ▲

Acanceh ▲   Xel-Ha ▲

▲ Mayapán   Cobá ▲

▲ Uxmal ▲ Maní   Tulum ▲   Cozumel

▲ Kabáh

▲ Sayil ▲ Xlabpac

Santa Rosa ▲ Labná
Xtampak ▲

▲ Nocuchic

Etzná ▲

El Tabasqueño ▲

▲ Hochob

Dzibanché
▲

Becam ▲ ▲ Xpuhil

Kohunlich
Chicaná ▲ ▲   ▲

Río Bec   Santa Rita

Itzamkanac   Xamantún ▲   ▲ Corozal

▲   Calakmul   Altún Ha ▲

▲ Lamanai

Balakbal ▲

Naachtún ▲ ▲ Xultún   ▲ La Honradez

Uaxactún ▲   ▲ Holmul

Piedras   Nakum ▲ Yaxhá ▲   **BELIZE**
Negras

Tikal ▲ Chunhuitz ▲ ● Belmopan   **CARIBBEAN SEA**

Yaxchilán ▲   Tayasal ▲ ▲ Benque Viejo

Bonampak ▲   ▲ Seibal ▲ El Naranjo

San Clemente   ▲ Xunantunich
Altar de
Sacrificios ▲   ▲ Lubaantún

▲ Pusilhá

Chamá ▲   Cancúen

GUATEMALA

Nebaj   San Agustín   Quiriguá
▲   ▲ Acasahuastlán ▲

▲ Iximché   ▲ Mixco Viejo   **HONDURAS**
                      ▲ Copán

Abaj   Kaminaljuyú ▲
Takalik ▲

El Baúl ▲   ● Guatemala

Santa Lucía ▲
Cotzumalhuapa

EL SALVADOR

● San Salvador

Campeche ●

Jaina ▲

Printed in:
Repeticiones Gráficas, S.A. de C.V.
Juárez 18-A, Tlacopac, San Ángel
01040 México, D.F.
2000 copies. February, 1997